MW00696149

Lead the

Young

People

▮ ▮ ▮

WITNESS LEE

LIVING STREAM MINISTRY
Anaheim, California • www.lsm.org

ISBN 0-7363-1034-7

Living Stream Ministry
2431 W. La Palma Ave., Anaheim, CA 92801
P. O. Box 2121, Anaheim, CA 92814 USA

00 01 02 03 04 05 / 9 8 7 6 5 4 3 2 1

HOW TO LEAD
YOUNG PEOPLE

Published in Chinese in 1963,
The Ministry of the Word, *Vol. 7, pp. 500-518.*
(Notes of fellowship on service in the church
in Taipei, not reviewed by the speaker)

The brothers asked me to give a word of fellowship tonight particularly to the brothers and sisters who serve in the young people's or students' work. The brothers would also like to have the brothers and sisters who serve in various homes participate in this fellowship. Therefore, tonight I am not giving a message; rather, I want to fellowship with you some principles concerning how to help the young people.

SEEING THE PRECIOUSNESS
OF THE YOUNG PEOPLE

In whatever a person does, the most important thing is to have a heart. Without a heart, a person will not want to do anything, and even if he does something, he will not be enthusiastic in doing it. Of course, this is also true with the young people's work. If you want to do this work, you must like the young people, care for them, and be concerned about their affairs. This may be considered the minimum "capital" required for the young people's work. If you have no interest in the young people and have no heart for them, doing the young people's work only out of reluctance, then it is useless.

Sometimes our heart may arise from our preference. When we like something, naturally we will have a heart to do it. Sometimes the heart we have may come from our knowledge. When we see the importance and value of a certain matter, we will spontaneously have a heart for it. According to my observation of the real situation among us concerning the young people's work, I see that some brothers and sisters are doing it out of their preference. Because they are naturally inclined to the young people and they enjoy contacting the young people, they come to do the young people's work. We cannot say that this is wrong. We have to admit that no matter how much grace we have received and how great the spirituality we possess, we are still human—we still have the part that is human. But here we have to say that it is not weighty enough to do the young people's work with such a heart. If we truly want to do the young people's work, and do it in a weighty manner, we must let God open our eyes to see the preciousness of the young people and their importance in God's hands. If we see this, we will appreciate this work, and spontaneously we will have a heart within us for it.

THE FUTURE OF THE LORD'S WORK DEPENDING ALTOGETHER ON THE YOUNG PEOPLE

If we read through the Bible carefully, we will discover a fact: It is not easy to find a case showing that God called an old person to do a new thing or a thing of great consequence. This may discourage the older brothers and sisters, but it is something undeniable. Indeed, we cannot see that God ever called an old person to do a new thing. Seemingly, Moses received God's call when he was eighty years old, but if we carefully read the Bible, we will see that actually the first time he received God's call was not when he was eighty years old. Rather, when he was still young, God's calling had already begun in him. If you read on, whether it was Joshua, Caleb, Samuel, or David in the Old Testament, or whether it was the twelve disciples called by the Lord Jesus in the New Testament, when they were first gained by the Lord, none of them was an old man. Not only is this true in the Bible, but even in all of church history it is hard to find a strong illustration to show that God called an old man when He had a new and important thing to do. We can say that virtually everyone used by God to begin a new thing or chosen by God to turn the age was a young man.

I would like to give you a testimony. Thirty years ago the Lord's work in China had a new beginning. In that period of time God did not call any old people. All the ones who are around fifty years old and who are standing firmly to serve before the Lord today were still young people who, thirty years ago, were around twenty years old. They were raised up by the Lord in the schools for that new work. Brothers and sisters, if you see this, you will treasure the young people before God.

Furthermore, nearly every work that the young people were called by God to do was a work that turned the age. God called Moses to turn one age, and He called Joshua to turn another age. Obviously, His calling of Samuel turned another age. The prophethood, priesthood, and kingship all hung on this young man Samuel. He was truly one who turned the age. David was also one who turned the age. Furthermore, we can see that Daniel and his three friends were young ones among the people in captivity. Through them God turned that age of captivity. Then in the New Testament, the first to emerge was John the Baptist. We know that he was a young man called by the Lord. God used him to turn the age at his time. We can go on to look at Paul, who was an apostle especially used by God. The Bible says that he was a young man when he was visited by the Lord (Acts 7:58). We all admit that Paul was a man who turned the age. I dare not overstate the case, but my feeling is that the work which the Lord started among us in the East thirty years ago also considerably bore the nature and element of an age-turning work. For the carrying out of all these works of great consequences, God always called young men.

I would like to tell you, brothers and sisters, that because we saw this, we have been paying much attention to the young people's work for nearly twenty years. This is not to say that one young person's soul is worth two older persons' souls. This is not what I mean. What I am saying is that a person has to be gained by the Lord at a young age if he will have some usefulness in God's hands or a future in God's work. This is an obvious fact.

Not only is this shown in the Bible and confirmed in church history, but it is even seen in all of human society. You have never seen old people being trained to start any new project or any new move. There is no school that solely accepts elderly students, nor is there any training center established exclusively for old people. Concerning this matter, I have to ask especially the older brothers and sisters to forgive me. There may be a seventy-year-old brother here who truly loves the Lord, and you may want to spend some time to help him. However, you will find out that it is a very difficult thing to do. You may tell him something in the morning, and he forgets it before noon. You may have clearly explained something in the morning, but in the afternoon he asks, "What is that all about?" He has forgotten again. His heart is fully burdened, but his mind is no longer fully competent. This is a cruel fact, but we cannot deny it.

Quite often I have said that for salvation, for the receiving of grace, and for the enjoyment of the Lord's salvation the older ones are absolutely precious. However, for usefulness in the Lord's hand, for the spread of the Lord's kingdom, and for the propagation of the Lord's work, the responsibility undoubtedly falls on the shoulders of the young people. If the Lord delays His coming back for five, ten, fifteen, or twenty years and He wants to accomplish something, the commission will have to be entrusted to the young people. Concerning those of us who are already over fifty, we all hope that we may be alive to see the Lord come back and not have to pass through the Jordan River of death. Nevertheless, we have to admit that the conditions today, such as the "greenness of the crops," the desolation of the church, and the scarcity of overcomers, tell us that the Lord cannot come back so soon. It is not that the Lord does not want to come back. Rather, He desperately wants to come back soon, but our condition does not allow Him. Therefore, seeing such a situation, we believe that there may be still a considerable amount of time in which the Lord wants to accomplish something on the earth.

Of course, we should also believe that the Lord may come back tomorrow. Nearly two thousand years ago He already said, "Behold, I come quickly!" In His estimation a thousand years are like one day; with Him there is no time element. On our side, however, if the Lord delays, I cannot believe that a number of us who are now over fifty will still be alive thirty years later. Some of the brothers and sisters are even older than I am and are in their sixties, and others are in their seventies. In any case, if the Lord delays His coming back, I am afraid we cannot wait that long and will all be gone. May I ask, who then will continue to do the Lord's work? You may be very spiritual, even too spiritual, and say, "The Lord will be responsible for all these matters." Of course, this is true; the Lord will be responsible. There is no denying this. But one thing is clear: Whether He takes direct responsibility or He wants you or me to do something for Him, the way is with the young people. Twenty years from now those who will be useful to the Lord are those who are in their twenties or younger today.

It is a universally accepted fact that a person receives education for twenty-five years, gains experience for another twenty-five years, and then becomes truly useful in the final twenty-five years. Three twenty-five years make a total of seventy-five years. I hope all our young people will live for seventy-five years—twenty-five years to receive spiritual education, another twenty-five years to gain spiritual experience, and the final twenty-five years to be used by God. I also hope that those who are in their fifties now will take good care of their health for the Lord's sake. However, brothers and sisters, please consider: Unless there is a group of young people who are saved to receive proper spiritual help today, how can they gain the experience and be used by the Lord in the future? If there are no young people gained by the Lord today, after our departure there will be no one to succeed us. Then there will be a gap.

Let me give you a testimony. Thirty years ago when the Lord raised us up in China, it was truly a hard time for us. Since there was no one who could help us in our service, we had to strenuously grope around in every matter. At that time we had left Christianity behind; therefore, even in the matter of how to meet we had to feel our way around little by little. Now, after more than thirty years, the young people then have become old people. If the Lord does not have a group of young people today to receive help, after some time, when we pass away, will there not be a gap? This will not only delay the day of the Lord but also diminish the effectiveness of our work. If there are young brothers and sisters raised up by the Lord, and if we are preserved to give them an absolutely positive leading instead of erroneous limitations, then there is no need to wait until the Lord takes us away; even today they can become useful in the Lord's hands.

We already saw this clearly more than twenty years ago. Therefore, from that time on we paid a great deal of attention to gaining the young intellectuals in the universities and hospitals. Thank the Lord, this work had good progress from 1936. The Lord gained a good number of young people from the Union Medical College in Peking, from a certain hospital in Tientsin, from the Ch'i Lu University in Tsinan, from the College of Nursing in Shanghai, and from some universities in Nanking. Many young medical students, resident physicians, nurses, and even professors became our brothers and sisters. About ten years later, among us nearly all the co-workers and responsible ones in the churches all over the country were the young people gained at that time. Therefore, after the War of Resistance against Japan [1937-1945] was won and the country was restored, then the Lord brought us back to Shanghai where there was a small work of revival again in the regions of Nanking and Shanghai. At that time we concentrated nearly seventy to eighty percent of our efforts on the young people. Within those two to three years all the work among the college students received much blessing from the Lord. Many young ones were gained by Him. By saying this much, I hope that the brothers and sisters can see the importance of the young people's work. This should create a heart in us to appreciate the young brothers and sisters.

I would say to you, brothers and sisters, that I love the older ones. The Lord can testify for me about this. But I also would ask the older ones to forgive me because I would also say that I really appreciate the young people's work. Some spread words about me saying that Brother Lee only cares for the young people's work and that he has chased all the older ones out to the street. I deny this; I never had that intention. However, for the future of the Lord's work, I would ask the older ones to pray much for the young people. The future of the work and the usefulness in the future, no doubt, are with the young people. From the view of saving souls, we should treat older ones and younger ones equally. From the view of the future of the work, however, we should put our emphasis on the younger ones. If the church or the work fails to gain young people, it will be like a family that has only some childless old people: an old grandfather who is eighty-five years old, a father who is sixty years old, and a son who is nearly forty years old. There are no younger ones under them; there are no crying ones or shouting ones. Rather, everyone is well-behaved. This is abnormal.

Sometimes when someone says to me, "Brother Lee, it seems that our church is in a mess and is not very orderly," I would say, "That is actually a good sign." When you visit a family, if you see some are crying, some are shouting, some are fighting, some are doing somersaults, and some are rolling on the floor, that is a good sign; it indicates that the family is flourishing. If a family has only an eighty-five year old grandfather, a sixty-year-old father, and a forty-year-old son, certainly no one will be rolling on the floor. Even if any of them desires to roll on the floor, he would not have the strength to do it. Therefore, all year round they live in quietness, orderliness, and loneliness. Brothers and sisters, we can be sure that such a family does not have to sell its house; the house will become someone else's house before long. In the same manner, when you visit a church, if you see throngs of young people there, then you should praise the Lord that the church has a future. You do not need to ask whether those young people are good or bad. Just as in a family, it does not matter how naughty the children are; they are still better than none. If there are no children, the family is doomed to hopelessness. Some children who are undesirable today may become desirable tomorrow. There is always hope.

In summary, we need to gain the young

people in the church and in the Lord's work. Anyone who works for the Lord with insight needs to pay attention to this matter. If you see this, your heart will be burdened to love the young people regardless of whether they are good or bad. Having a young one who is not very desirable is better than having none at all. May the brothers and sisters as the Lord's lovers all love the young people for the future of the church and for the Lord's work.

Concerning the practical side, we will mention the following points.

HAVING AN INTEREST
IN THE YOUNG PEOPLE

First of all, I have already said this earlier, but now I want to say it again: If you want to help the young people, you must have an interest in them. I was in a place where there was a group of brothers and sisters who were forty and fifty years of age. None of them had anything good to say about the young people. Some of them told me, "Brother Lee, look at the young people among us. Do they look proper?

They don't know the difference between the elderly and the young, between seniors and juniors. They give us a cold shoulder when they see us on the street. They stare at us when they see us at the entrance of the meeting hall. Brother Lee, you have to give a message to render some help to these young people so that they will know the difference between seniors and juniors, between the elderly and the young." At another time a brother in his fifties came to see me and said, "Brother Lee, look at the young people among us. They are so improper. When they walk, their steps are flying and their eyes are wandering. They are really out of order." Some time later while I was with a group of elderly brothers, one of them asked me to give a message that would teach the young people to be obedient. He said, "Our young people simply do not obey the elderly ones." That day I felt it was a good opportunity to say a word to them. Therefore, I said, "Brothers, you have mentioned to me many times how wrong the young people are. I would like to ask you, if the young people are right, then what need is there for you, the older ones? No doubt they are wrong, but what kind of example have you given them?" I spoke at some length to them that day with the intention to incite them to help the young people and have an interest in them. Do not find their faults at first. If you do, you cannot help them.

Some have a special liking for the young people whom they consider good, but they purse their mouths and shake their heads when they see those whom they think are not good. This is wrong. Often times God will prove to you that your evaluation of those whom you think are good is inaccurate. Instead, those whom you consider not good may be greatly used by God. Therefore, it is hard to say that those whom we feel are good now will be good in the future, and those whom we feel are bad today will be bad tomorrow. We should never trust in our own judgment. This applies even to our evaluation of ourselves. We may be good today, but that does not guarantee that we will be good to the end. We may be bad today, but the Lord may turn us to be good tomorrow. Likewise, regardless of whether the young people are good or bad, we need to treat everyone the same, and we need to like them and be concerned for them. Do they walk as if they are flying? Then you should fly with them. Are their eyes wandering? You should also let your eyes wander. Are they playing ball? Play a game with them, and then talk to them about the Lord Jesus when the game is over. This is genuine capability. However, if you cannot talk to them about the Lord Jesus because He is gone after you play ball, then your spirituality is false.

Let me give you another example. Suppose you run into a young brother on the street. You ask him where he is going, and he says, "I am going to a movie because I am very bored." Never rebuke him with a long face, saying, "Why are you going to watch a movie? How can you do that?" If you do this, you will not be able to help this young man. It is better for you to have a little conversation with him. Ask him what movie and which theater he is going to. Then walk with him for a short distance or call a taxi and ride with him. While you are on the way to the theater,

you can talk to him about
things that are on your hea
ask him, "Brother, did you e
the Word in the last couple o.
this way you can begin to tal.
about reading the Bible. You can a
to him about prayer and ask him
has prayed recently. When you get to
theater, you may tell him, "Brother, he
we are. You go in, and I'll pay for the tax.
I have to go to a meeting. Ten minutes
before the end of the movie I will come
back and be here waiting for you." Instead
of being impatient with him, you are fully
interested in him. If you have some money
with you, you may ask him, "Brother, do
you have your cash ready? Is it enough to
buy the ticket? If not, I can give you some."
Brothers and sisters, if you can do this,
see whether or not you can lead him! I
am afraid that you may be like a "lawyer"
with an expressionless face, teaching him
sternly and even condemning him. After
being condemned by you, he may not be
able to be delivered from movies for the
rest of his life—he will not be able to live
without watching movies. His going to the

es for the rest of his life will be due
our provoking. Do not think that I
talking nonsense. I know what I am
king about.

This is what the Lord Jesus did that
ay on the way to Emmaus. The Lord
asked the two disciples, saying, "What are
these words which you are exchanging
with one another while you are walking?"
(Luke 24:17). One of them replied, "Do You
alone dwell as a stranger in Jerusalem and
not know the things which have taken
place in it in these days?" (v. 18). Of course,
the Lord Jesus was very clear, but He still
asked them, "What things?" (v. 19). They
talked a great deal, and the Lord Jesus
just listened patiently. They were walking
downhill, and the Lord Jesus just walked
with them. In the end, however, the Lord
opened their eyes, and they turned around.
Brothers and sisters, I believe that you all
know what I mean by these words. Do you
want to help the young people? Then, first
of all you need to be interested in them.
Do not be concerned first about their
mistakes; do not condemn them at all. You
should give them a feeling that you are

their good friend, that you sympathize with them, and that you are interested in them and in their affairs. This is the chief point.

DOING YOUR BEST TO CONTACT THE YOUNG PEOPLE

Second, learn to do your best to contact the young people. Helping the young brothers and sisters depends not on your ability to give them messages but on your regular, frequent contacts with them. When you contact the young brothers and sisters, do not begin by asking, "How many chapters of the Bible have you read today? Have you prayed?" Such questions should not be brought up until you have had many contacts with them, maybe even after eight or ten times. Remember not to talk about spiritual things at the initial contact with them. It is even more so in dealing with an unbeliever. Do not talk about the Lord Jesus when you first contact him. The reason you refrain from mentioning the Lord Jesus is that as you maintain contact with him, seemingly you are retreating, yet actually you are advancing.

21

You need to sense his feeling until one day you can impart the gospel into him. Then you will be successful at once. However, if you do it prematurely, it is easy to cause a negative reaction. If you mess up the whole thing, he may not receive the Lord for his entire lifetime. It is the same in dealing with any young person. Do not stir up his negative feeling by talking to him right away about reading the Bible or praying. You must wait until you have more contacts with him and he feels that he likes you and that you also like him. Once you have touched his feeling and earned his trust, then you can begin to talk about spiritual things. This is like giving the right prescription for an illness. With the right medicine, the illness will be cured. Then you can expect to see a result.

EMPHASIZING PRACTICALITY INSTEAD OF STRESSING DOCTRINES

Third, when you help the young people, do not give them a lot of doctrines; instead, give them something practical. You should not put too much emphasis on doctrines, not only when you have personal contact with them but also when you are preaching the gospel or giving messages to them. If you give them only some doctrines and they come only to listen, there will not be much effect. The more you speak doctrines, the more the young people become dead, cold, and backsliding. Because young people have many practical problems, you need to sense their feelings beginning with these problems. Therefore, you need to spend some time to study the problems of the young people in their practical living, including problems both before and after their salvation. Based upon your studies, when you preach the gospel or speak a word of edification to them, what you speak is practical and is related to the practical matters that you have touched in their lives.

HAVING A POSITIVE FAITH IN EVERY YOUNG PERSON

Fourth, you need to have positive faith in every young person. This means that with the good ones you should believe that they will get better, and with the ones who do not seem to be good, you should also believe that they will become good. Moreover, you should have more faith in those who are seemingly not good and believe that they will become good and not have as much faith in those who are good.

I like to tell you, brothers and sisters, that we are all Adam's descendants, a fallen race. Even the children of godly people are fallen. We cannot say that to be fallen is right, but please remember that all those who truly know God's salvation were once fallen people. If a person has been preserved since his birth and has never lived in a fallen way, he cannot have a deep experience of God's salvation. One who has never lived in a fallen way cannot experience God's salvation. I am not encouraging people to be fallen. Neither am I encouraging them to be loose with their children. This is not what I mean. What I mean is that you should never think that it is all right to despise certain young ones simply because they are not good. This concept is wrong.

We know the story of George Müller, a spiritual man in the nineteenth century. He was clear about his salvation probably when he was twenty-one years old. He was born into a Christian family, and his father was a man who feared God. However, he was a very fallen young man before the age of twenty-one. He always stole money from his father to roam about from place to place. Once he stayed in a hotel, but because he was not able to pay the fee, he was even sent to prison by the owner of the hotel. At that time he was truly a dissipated and corrupt person. But one day the Lord found him. As a young man, after he was saved, he became one who greatly loved the Lord. If you look at George Müller before he was twenty-one, he was such an improper person. Who could ever have imagined that after he was twenty-one he would love the Lord so much and be so spiritual? Therefore, you cannot judge a young person's future based on his situation today.

Brothers and sisters, I can tell you that whether the condition of the young people is good or bad, usually it is not trustworthy. Today you may consider a certain young man very bad, but one day he may become very good, contrary to your view. In the same way, today you may think that a certain young man is very good, but some day he may become very bad. Therefore, all those who have some experience in the young people's work will say, "We don't trust in the young people's condition. On the positive side, however, we fully believe that God will gain them one day." This will deliver us so that we will not work only on the young people whom we consider good and put aside those whom we consider bad. Actually, sometimes it is hard for those who are consistently good to have spiritual perception, and often their growth is slow. However, if you spend time on those seemingly bad ones to turn them around, their spiritual understanding will be opened immediately after they have made a turn. This shows that those of us who do the work among the young people should not trust in their present condition. Do not believe either in their good condition or in their bad condition; believe only in God's work. No matter how bad one may be, we still believe God's work can turn him. No matter how poor one may be, we still believe God's work can carry him through. Because we have such a positive faith, we pay attention to every young person.

ADAPTING TO YOUNG PEOPLE

Fifth, all those who have a desire to do the young people's work need to learn how to match and adapt to the young people. Do not ask them to adapt to you. You need to adapt to them to such an extent that you are like glue. Glue adapts the best; there is not one place it cannot adapt to. It adapts to flat surfaces, rugged places, twisted places, and places with corners. Glue can be applied to any place. We who do the young people's work need to deal with our character to such an extent that we are just like glue. If anyone wants to serve God, he must have a character that is not only strong but also pliant; he must be one who tempers strength with pliancy to adapt to others like glue.

For example, young people are facing stiff competition for the entrance to a higher school, and there is a prevailing atmosphere to go abroad to study. After elementary school, they have to enter high school. Then after high school, they have to get into a university. After graduation from university, they have to go abroad to further their studies. Everyone is busy getting a higher education and going abroad. It seems very hard to do the young people's work because the young people are too busy to care about pursuing the Lord. But this perception is not accurate. We who do the young people's work should be like glue, so that it does not matter if a young person is soft or hard or if he is three-dimensional, flat, or a surface with bumps and dents; we still need to stick to him. We have to go along with the young people and accommodate ourselves to them. Are they busy with entering a higher school? Then we work on them by going along with them in their preparation for this matter. Are they going abroad to study? We still go along with them and adapt to them. Although we cannot go with any of them to a foreign country, our care and concern for him will go with him. We should work not only to the extent of gaining him but also to gain some people through him in that foreign country. We should work on him to such an extent that he will do the Lord's work in whatever university he goes to. Then as a result of his preaching of the gospel, he will gain some people there. Therefore, instead of regarding the prevailing trend of going abroad as a hindrance, we should consider it an outlet for our work. We need to correspond with the brothers and sisters who are studying abroad to continue communication with them. Before they leave, we need to lead each of them to have a normal spiritual life, so that after they go out they will not only study for themselves but also work for the Lord. You cannot, and must not, hope that everyone would give up entering a higher school or going abroad for further studies but would sit here waiting for you to work on them, just like a piece of tofu placed on a plate for you to eat. This is not called work. If we are doing a real work, then even if a young person flies to the sky, we will follow him there to adapt to him.

Many say that students today are too busy. However, if you really know the students' situation, you will know that with the young people, being busy is not a problem. Rather, the real issue is their interest. If they are interested in something, no matter how busy they are, they will have time for it. They will find time for the things they are interested in even if they are busy.

At the apostles' time, the Roman Empire persecuted Christians. The Roman Caesar, the emperor, killed many Christians. However, the apostles were very effective. They were able to work to such an extent that even some who were in Caesar's household were saved. Philippians 4:22 says, "All the saints greet you, and especially those of Caesar's household." This proves that the apostles worked even into Caesar's home.

Therefore, we must remember that in doing the Lord's work we must not be rigid. We should not say that we can eat only tofu and not stones. A competent worker can eat not only tofu but also stones, and he can eat something even as hard as diamonds. Brothers and sisters, please believe me; learn to adapt to others.

PAYING ATTENTION
TO PERSONAL CONTACT

Sixth, all those who care for the work among the young people must pay attention to doing a personal work. The power and effect of doing a personal work with the young people are many times greater than the meetings. Big meetings do not have much effect on young people; individual contact is most effective. When you gather them together, usually all you can do is give them a message and at most a little work of revival. The emphasis of a genuine work with young people is individual contact. If you ask me, "Brother Lee, how would you do the young people's work?" I would answer you by saying, "I can do it without holding any big meetings from the beginning to the end of the year but just absolutely working with them individually by personal contact." It seems this way is fragmentary and wastes a lot of time. You may be able to contact only one person in an hour, and sometimes you may not be able to contact even one person after half a day. It seems time is pitifully wasted. Seemingly, this way is less effective than holding big meetings where you can speak to hundreds of people at once. Rather, experience tells us that holding big meetings is useless. If you hold big meetings all year round, there may not be much result. All you gain will be some shallow ones. Please remember, however, if you pay attention to individual contact, although you may not gain one person in a month or may gain only one person in two months, each one who is gained through your personal contact counts. Moreover, like you, he will contact others. You have gained one, but eventually this one will become two, two will become four, four will become eight, and eight will become sixteen, and every one of them will be solid. After some time you will see a great number of people gained.

I hope that all the ones doing the young students' work, whether it is bringing them to salvation, helping them to be spiritual, or leading them to preach the gospel, will pay attention to individual contact. From 1946 to 1948, when we were in the regions of Shanghai and Nanking, we did not actually have any students' meetings or young people's meetings. Most of our work was carried out by individual contact, yet the result was quite good. If the brothers neglect individual contact and pay attention only to young people's meetings, I can say with certainty that after having so many meetings, the young people's work will end up with something that is only on the surface, like loose sand without foundation. It will not be able to produce any solid ones. If you want to produce solid ones, you must have personal contact. You must not be disappointed with anyone; rather, you would spend time to contact everyone individually.

Of course, in the matter of personal contact, skills are needed. But if you practice this matter seriously, gradually you will gain experience and insight. You will know which one among so many young people should be contacted and gained first. Later, after that one has been gained by the Lord, one thing is sure: Since you stirred him up in this way, he will go to stir others up in the same way. This is just like a machine with so many gear wheels;

when one wheel turns, all the other wheels also turn. In this way, one by one will be affected, just like the unending multiplication of offspring. Therefore, you can see that even if there are no big meetings, many can still get saved and many can still be raised up to love the Lord. That is the time when you can begin to hold big meetings, and no matter what you speak they will receive it. Then the meetings will be one hundred percent effective. You will be able to gain solid young people and do a deep work in them.

When you have personal contact with young people, on the one hand, you need to have broad contact with them, treating every one of them equally; on the other hand, you need to have specific contact. What I mean by specific contact is that you need to exercise your spiritual insight and follow the Spirit's leading to sense which ones, among so many young students, you should lead to the Lord first. Then you should spend your effort on them to help them receive the Lord's salvation. In the same way, among so many young brothers and sisters, you need to feel and see which ones, once they are gained, will have impact on others. Then you should spend your effort on them first and help them to love and pursue the Lord. Once they are raised up, they will influence the other young brothers and sisters.

Therefore, in doing the work among the young people, on the one hand, you need to have broad contact with them, dealing with them in a general way; on the other hand, you need to have specific contact, helping the ones who can take the lead and influence others. If you gain one, I repeat, he will go and help others without your teaching him. Because you have helped him in this way, you will go to help others in the same way. As a result, one will become two, two will become four, and so on. This is like the ripple effect achieved by throwing a stone in the center of the water. The ripple will eventually spread to cover the entire surface of the lake. Then you can hold big meetings, and they will be effective. If you hold big meetings from the outset, there will be only a twenty percent effect, and the other eighty percent will amount to zero. If you are willing to start from individual contact and then go on to big meetings, the messages you give will be practical and the work you do will produce a hundred percent result.

All the points above are some of the experiences I have gained from touching the young people's work in the past years. Any matter has its own intricacy and requires experience. In particular, matters such as leading people to salvation, helping people to love the Lord, and bringing people to serve the Lord are very deep and very fine, consisting of many intricate points. Yes, it is the Spirit's work, but we all know that the Spirit needs the proper ones to coordinate with Him. Some can coordinate with the Spirit, but others cannot. Some are useful in the hands of the Spirit, but others are useless. We need to pay attention and study these matters when we start to do this work.

These six points which I have fellowshipped with you all are just an introduction. If you will take this fellowship and go on, you will learn more and make more progress. You will find better ways to lead the young people to the Lord to receive His salvation.

Brothers, I say again, the Lord has a great need for the young people. This generation needs many young people to rise up in a strong way to receive the Lord's salvation and be led by the Lord to become useful vessels in His hands. May the Lord be gracious to us that in His work and in the church we will treasure the souls of the young people. Not only will we not hinder them or damage them, but we will aggressively attract them, perfect them, lead them, and cultivate them so that they will experience the Lord's salvation and receive the Lord's building up to become useful ones in the Lord's hands. I truly hope that all the brothers and sisters will pray faithfully for this matter before the Lord for the future of the Lord's work.